D0347261

Aural Time!

HULL COLLEGE LIBRARY
CLASS 782 TUR
I.S.B.N. 1844497070
BAR CODE 000223074
LOC QG

Practice Tests for ABRSM and other Exams

Grade 6

DAVID TURNBULL

CONTENTS

Introduction ii

Test A: Singing or Playing from Memory 1

Test B: Sight Singing 9

Test C: Perfect and Imperfect Cadences 24

Test D: Questions about Pieces 28

Appendix: Comments on Test D 38

Check for CD
on Issue and Return

* 000223074 *

INTRODUCTION

Aural training has always been of the greatest importance to teachers and their pupils. In recent years the emphasis has changed from dependence on memory to the development of a wider sense of musical awareness.

The Associated Board of the Royal Schools of Music revised its aural tests for Grades 1–5 in 1993 (with some further changes in Grades 4 and 5 in 1995). New tests are being introduced for Grades 6–8 from January, 1996.

Like most musical skills, aural awareness needs regular training and practice. Aural work should be part of every lesson. Teachers may like to use this book to supplement the aural training material they devise for themselves.

The 1996 tests for Grade 6 include tests in accompanied sight-singing. This most important musical skill — the basis of so much musical training and enjoyment — has been neglected in musical education in the last few decades. Pupils will need considerable practice to achieve the necessary standard, and it is hoped that the large number of sight-singing tests in this volume will be helpful. Most of the material has been transferred from the original edition of *Aural Time!* Grade 5, following the decision of the ABRSM to abandon accompanied sight-singing at Grade 5 level in 1995. Pupils may be also find another book in the *Aural Time!* series useful. *Easy Sight Singing & Voice Pitching Practice*, (Bosworth Edition 4801), contains 70 short examples of accompanied sight-singing suitable for a beginner, in a variety of major and minor keys.

The material in this book will be found useful not only for ABRSM examinations. The skills developed by its use will be of considerable help to candidates for GCSE and A level, and for all musicians who wish to improve their general musical awareness.

Most of the examples in this book have been taken from the works of established composers. In many cases examples have been adapted or transposed to make them more useful for their present purpose. As always, I am grateful to my wife for her constant help and encouragement.

David Turnbull
Solihull, June 1995

Uniform with this volume: *Aural Time!* Grades 1–5 (already published). Pupil's book for Grades 4 & 5. *Aural Time!* Grades 7 and 8 in preparation.

Also by David Turnbull: *Theory Time!* Step-by-step instruction in musical theory and rudiments. Grades 1–5.

All published by Bosworth & Co.

Test A. Singing or Playing from Memory

Pupils must sing or play from memory the upper part of a two-part phrase. The key-chord and the starting note will be played and named, and two bars of the pulse will be tapped.

In an examination, the example will be played twice. When giving practice, however, teachers should not hesitate to play the test more frequently, and if necessary be prepared to divide the test into sections. Tests should be played at the keyboard using both hands, so that the separate lines are as clearly defined as possible. *If the example starts with a single part or a unison, the pupil must be warned.*

© 1995 by Bosworth & Co. Ltd., London

International Copyright Secured

Allegro non troppo
Easter Hymn
6
mf
Allegro non troppo
Purcell
7
f
Andantino sans lenteur
Debussy
8
pp
Andante
Schütz
9
mf
Corelli
10
mp
Allegro
Handel
11
f
Andante
Mozart
12
p

Grazioso
Brahms
13
mf
Adagio
Haydn
14
p
Allegro
Schumann
15
mf
sf
Andante
D. Scarlatti
16
p
Andante
Bach
17
f
Moderato
Gibbons
18
mf
Andante
Lee
19
f

© 1968 Novello & Co. Ltd.

Adagio
Haydn
27
mf
Allegretto non troppo
Berlioz
28
f
Andante
Scottish traditional
29
mf
Andante
Beethoven
30
f
Andante
Mozart
31
f
Andante non troppo
Berlioz
32
mf
Andante
Bach
33
mf

Andante
Monteverdi
34
mf

Allegro alla marcia
Puccini
35
f

Allegro e staccato
Handel
36
f

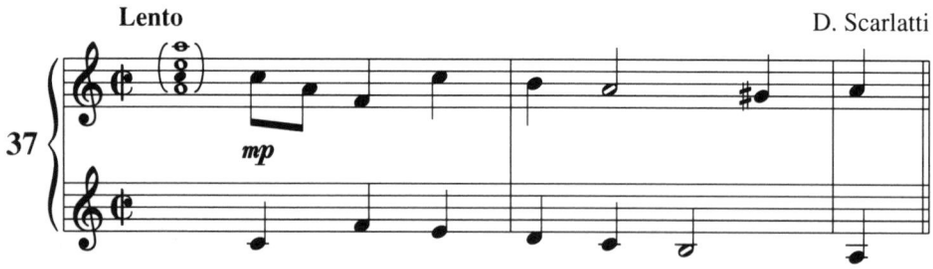
Lento
D. Scarlatti
37
mp

Allegretto
Haydn
38
f

Allegro
Handel
39
f

Allegretto
Beethoven
40
p

Adagio
Susato
41
f
Tempo di Valse
Chopin
42
mf
Andante
Dvořák
43
mf
p
Lento, ma non troppo
Debussy
44
pp
Lento
Elgar
45
mf
Andante
Gounod
46
p
Andante
Czerny
47
p

Reproduced by permission of Boosey & Hawkes Music Publishers Ltd.

Reproduced by permission of Universal Edition (London) Ltd.

Test B. Sight-Singing

Pupils must sing a short melody from score, with an accompaniment being played for them. The key-chord and starting note will be sounded, and the pulse indicated. Grade 6 sight-singing can be in any major or minor key up to three sharps or three flats. In an examination, pupils may choose to sing either in the treble or the bass clef. When practising, however, pupils are advised to familiarise themselves with both clefs, singing the examples up or down an octave as necessary.

Andante
Ford: Since first I saw your face
5
mp
p
Andante
Torelli: Tu lo sai
6
p
p
Lento
Byrd: My Little Sweet Darling
7
p
p
Lento
Trad: Blow the wind southerly
8
mp
p legato

Moderato
Schubert: To Music
9
p
pp

Tempo di valse
J. Strauss: Morning Papers
10
mf
p

Andante
Mozart: Requiem
11
f
mf

Andante
Handel: Messiah
12
f
f
p

Purcell: *Dido and Aeneas*
Fast
13
f
f

Giordani: *Caro mio ben*
Larghetto
14
p
p dolce

Handel: *Judas Maccabeus*
Allegro
15
f
f
mp

J. Strauss: *Die Fledermaus*
Allegretto
16
p
mf
pp

Andante
from The Beggar's Opera
17
mf
p

Moderato
Schumann: Dichterliebe
18
p
p

Andante
A. Scarlatti: O Cessate di piargarmi
19
p
p

Andante
Spiritual: Steal Away
20
p
p

Purcell: *Dido and Aeneas*
Slow
21
mp
p
mp

Scarlatti: *Già il sole dal Gange*
Allegro
22
f
f

Tempo moderato
Bach: *Christmas Oratorio*
23
f
f

Andante
Mozart: *Requiem*
24
f
p

Handel: *See the Conquering Hero Comes*
Moderato
25
f
f

Allegretto
Lotti: *Par dicesti*
26
p
p

Moderato
Fauré: *Requiem*
27
p
p

Purcell: *Man is for the Woman made*
Allegro
28
f
f *non legato*

Allegro
Arne: Where the bee sucks
29
mp
mp
p
Lento
Offenbach: Orpheus in the Underworld
30
mf
mf
p
Allegro
Purcell: Nymphs and Shepherds
31
mf
mf
Andante larghetto
Handel: Messiah
32
p
cresc.
f
p
cresc.
f

Allegro
Purcell: *Aeolus' Song*
33
f
f

Larghetto
Handel: *Messiah*
34
mf
p

Sostenuto
Mendelssohn: *Elijah*
35
p
cresc.
f
cresc.

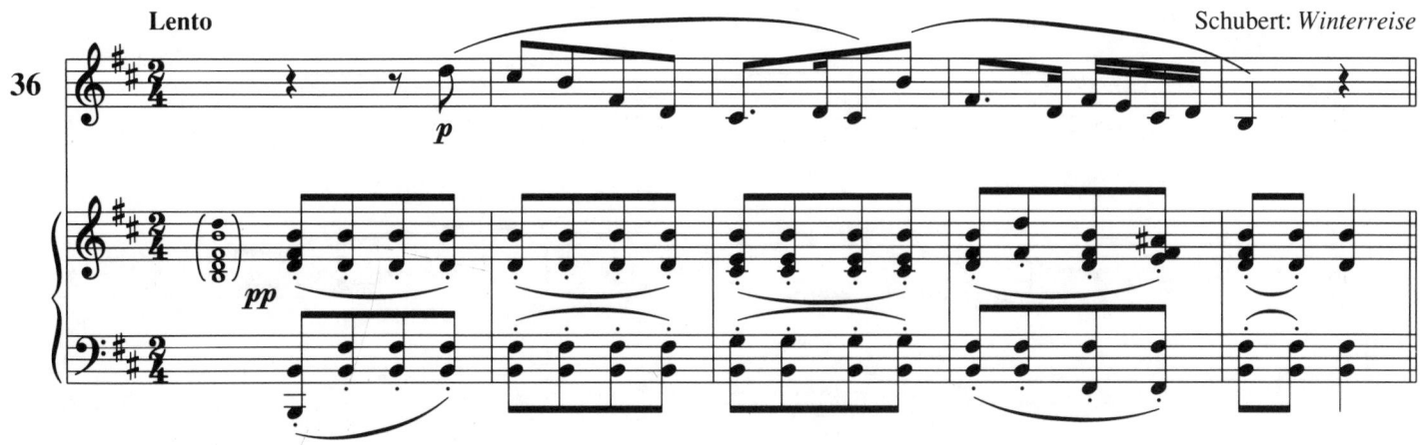
Lento
Schubert: *Winterreise*
36
p
pp

Largo
Handel: *Messiah*
37
mp
mp
p
mp

Andantino
Mendelssohn: *St. Paul*
38
p
p

Allegretto
Schubert: *Hark! Hark! the Lark*
39
p
p

Andante
Bach: *Jesu Joy of Man's Desiring*
40
mf legato
p
3
3
3

Lento
Schumann: *Dichterliebe*
41
f
f

Andante
Bach: *St. John Passion*
42
mf
p

Andantino
Elgar: *Dream of Gerontius*
43
pp
pp

Purcell: *Music for a while*
Lento
44
p
cresc.
dim.
p
p

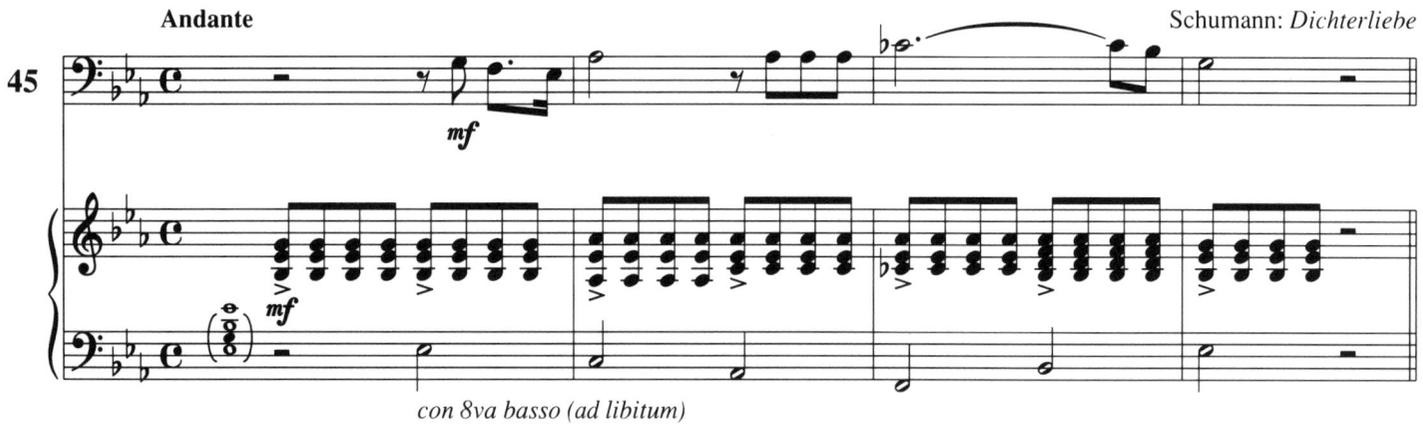
Andante
Schumann: Dichterliebe
45
mf
mf
con 8va basso (ad libitum)

Andante
Haydn: Creation
46
p
p

Lento
D'Urfey: Of a noble race
47
p
p

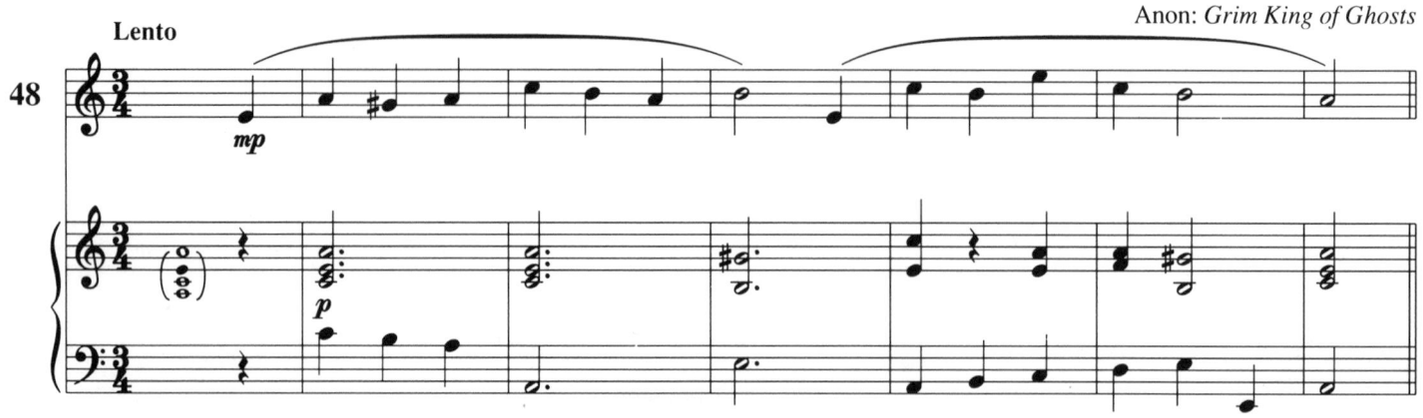
Lento
Anon: Grim King of Ghosts
48
mp
p

Anon: *Here's to the maiden*
Andante
49
mf
mf

Barrett: *Ianthe the lovely*
Lento
50
mp
mp

Schubert: *Lied*
Andante
51
p
p

Schubert: *Schäfers Klagelied*
Andante
52
pp
pp

Allegro
Schubert: *Who is Sylvia?*
53
mf
p

Largo ma non troppo
Handel: *Messiah*
54
f
mp

Monteverdi: *Lasciatemi morire*
Lento
55
p
mf
p

Adagio
Fauré: *Requiem*
56
p
p

Test C. Perfect and Imperfect Cadences.

(Pupils are advised to read over pages 20 – 21 of Theory Time! *Grade 5)*

In Grade 6 aural tests, pupils need only to be able to recognise **perfect and imperfect cadences**. A **perfect cadence** ends with the tonic chord, preceded by the dominant (or the dominant seventh) chord. An **imperfect cadence** ends with the dominant chord, preceded by any other chord. To be successful in Grade 6 cadence tests, pupils must be able to decide quickly if a phrase ends on the tonic chord (in which case the cadence is perfect), or on the dominant chord (in which case the cadence is imperfect).

In **major** keys, the tonic and dominant chords are both major chords. In **minor** keys, the tonic chord is minor, but the dominant chord is *major.* In Grade 6 tests, therefore, if a passage in a minor key ends with a major chord *the cadence must be imperfect.*

The key chord will always be sounded before a phrase is played over, so the pupil will know if the key of the phrase is major or minor. Teachers should ensure that the keychord is recognised correctly before continuing with the test.

A number of examples contain two cadences for identification. In some of these cases, the final chord of the first cadence is marked with a pause sign (fermata).

Allegretto
J. S. Bach
5
p
Andante
Byrd
6
Allegretto
Beethoven
7
f
Allegretto
Beethoven
8
f
S. Baring-Gould
9
Moderato
English traditional
10
Maestoso
J. Parry
11

Lento
German traditional
12
Andante grazioso
Mozart
13
p
sf
p
sf
p
Larghetto
Handel
14
mf
Andante
Beethoven
15
p
sf
Andante
Mozart
16
p
Andante maestoso
Mendelssohn
17
mf
3
sf

Allegro
Beethoven
18
pp
ff
Allegro
Offenbach
19
ff
Allegretto
Purcell
20
mp
Un poco andante
cantando
Grieg
21
pp
p
sim.
Grave
Dowland
22
mp
Andante
Verdi
23
p
pp
Lento
English traditional
24
p

Test D. Questions about Pieces

In Test D of ABRSM examinations the questions on pieces are in two parts.

D (i) Pupils should be able to answer questions about the **musical features** of a piece. These features include **rhythm**, **tempo** (including changes to tempo), **melody**, **form** (including phrase structure and phrase length), **tonality**, **dynamics** (including gradations of dynamics), **articulation** of notes, **harmony**, and **texture**. A consideration of these features should allow a pupil to determine the **character** of the music, and its **style** and **period**.

Only one or two questions will be chosen from the list printed below each piece, and the pupil will be told about which features will be the subject of questions before the piece is played.

Further information may be found on pages 10 – 12 of the Pupil's Book for Grades 4 and 5 of the *Aural Time!* series by David Turnbull (Bosworth Edition 4909).

Comments on the questions about pieces in this section are printed on Page 38.

D (ii) Pupils must clap a single-line extract taken from each piece, and be able to describe the piece as being in two, three, or four time. In examination situations, pupils will only be asked to clap one example, but to provide more practice two examples for clapping are given for each piece.

The questions in this section are useful preparation for many other types of music examination, like the GCSE. Pupils for other examinations can practise writing down *answers instead of giving them verbally.*

D (i) ***Questions***

(a) What do you notice about the **rhythm** of this piece?
(b) Is the **tonality** mostly major, or minor?
(c) Does the **tempo** alter, or stay the same?
(d) Is the **texture** homophonic (block chords), or polyphonic?
(e) Describe the **dynamics** of the piece.
(f) Comment on the relationship between the right hand and left hand **phrases** at the start.

D (ii) Clap one of the following extracts, and say if the piece is in two, three or four time.

D (i) ***Questions***

(a) Describe the **structure** of this piece.
(b) The piece is a dance. What is this type of dance called?
(c) Does the **tempo** alter, or stay the same?
(d) What do you notice about the bass of the **harmony** in the middle section?
(e) In which **historical period** might this have been written?

D (ii) Clap one of the following extracts, and say if the piece is in two, three or four time.

D (i) ***Questions***

(a) Comment on the **structure** of the melody in the first half of this piece.
(b) How long are most of the **phrase lengths**?
(c) Does the **tempo** alter, or stay the same?
(d) Is the **texture** homophonic (block chords), or polyphonic?
(e) Is the **tonality** mostly major, or minor? Does it change?

D (ii) Clap one of the following extracts, and say if the piece is in two, three or four time.

1 

2 

D (i) ***Questions***

(a) What does every two-bar **phrase** have in common?
(b) Describe the **dynamics** of the piece.
(c) Does the **tempo** alter? If so, how?
(d) Is the **texture** homophonic (block chords), or polyphonic?
(e) In what **period** might this have been written? Name a possible composer.

D (ii) Clap one of the following extracts, and say if the piece is in two, three or four time.

1

2

D (i) ***Questions***

(a) Is the **tonality** of the opening phrase major or minor?
(b) How often is the opening three-note **rhythmic** figure of the melody heard?
(c) Does the **tempo** alter?
(d) What do you feel is the **character** of this music?
(e) In what **period** might this have been written? Name a possible composer.

D (ii) Clap one of the following extracts, and say if the piece is in two, three or four time.

D (i) ***Questions***

(a) Is the **texture** of the music mostly polyphonic, or homophonic?
(b) Compare the opening **melody** with the first phrase in the bass.
(c) Does the **tempo** alter. If so, where?
(d) In what **period** might this have been written?

D (ii) Clap one of the following extracts, and say if the piece is in two, three or four time.

1

2

D (i) ***Questions***

(a) Comment on the type of **harmony** used in this piece.
(b) This piece is in the **style** of a dance. What sort of dance?
(c) Does the **tempo** alter? If so, how?
(d) What happens to the **dynamics** at the end?
(e) In what **period** might this have been written? Name a possible composer.

D (ii) Clap one of the following extracts, and say if the piece is in two, three or four time.

1 

2 

D (i) ***Questions***

(a) What is the **tonality** of the music in the first section? in the second section?
(b) This piece in the **style** of a dance. What sort of dance?
(c) What happens to the **tempo** in the second section?
(d) Describe the **dynamics** of the piece.
(e) In what **period** might this have been written?

D (ii) Clap one of the following extracts, and say if the piece is in two, three or four time.

D (i) ***Questions***

(a) Is the **tonality** of this major or minor?
(b) Is the **articulation** of the notes legato, staccato, or a mixture of both?
(c) Does the **tempo** vary? If so, where?
(d) What is the **character** of the music?
(e) In what musical **period** do you think it was written?

D (ii) Clap one of the following extracts, and say if the piece is in two, three or four time.

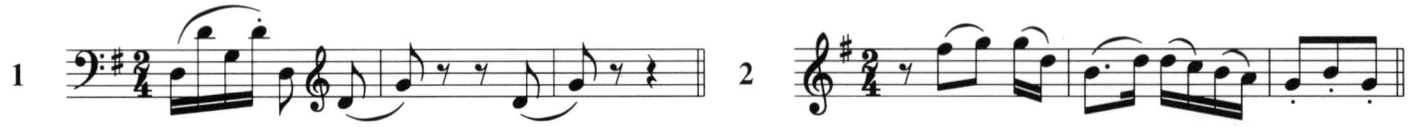

D (i) ***Questions***

(a) Is the **tonality** at the beginning of this major or minor?
(b) Comment on the respective **rhythms** of the hands in the first section.
(c) Describe any variations in **tempo**.
(d) Comment on the difference in **texture** between the two sections.
(e) In what musical **period** do you think it was written?

D (ii) Clap one of the following extracts, and say if the piece is in two, three or four time.

1

2

Appendix. Comments on the questions on music in Test D.

Pupils should read pages 10 – 12 in Aural Time! *Pupil's Book for Grades 4 & 5, noting the warning that generalisation about styles and periods is difficult and needs experience.*

The answers below are not the only possible ones.

No. 1 (a) Repetitive ♩. ♩♩ pattern, and some syncopation; (b) minor; (c) alters, as score; (d) polyphonic; (e) as score; (f) imitation at the octave.

No. 2 (a) AABA; (b) Minuet – minuets are in triple time and usually *allegretto*. Baroque minuets often start on the first beat of the bar, but classical and later ones on the third beat. (c) as score; (d) it consists of octave leaps on the same pitches (forming a 'pedal point'), using a repeating rhythmic figure; (e) straightforward harmony, lack of dissonance and balance of phrases all suggest classical period.

No. 3 (a) The phrases are almost the same apart from their ends – A, A^1, A, A^1; (b) 3 bars; (c) it stays the same; (d) polyphonic; (e) modulates to minor (D minor), also to C major.

No. 4 (a) the same rhythm; (b) as score; (c) as score; (d) harmonic; (e) frequent use of 7th chords, gradations in dynamics suggest (e) romantic period.

No. 5 (a) Minor; (b) 5 times; (c) no; (d) melancholy, though in a very restrained way; (e) classical period.

No. 6 (a) polyphonic, with much imitation; (b) it is similar but lower in pitch (imitation at the (compound) 4th below); (c) no; (d) answers to a, b and c, together with straightforward harmony, suggest baroque period.

No. 7 (a) Thick, rich chords (particularly parallel 7ths), with modal harmonies in the outer sections and chromatic notes in the middle; (b) sarabande – a sarabande is a slow dance in triple time, with a tendency to dwell on the second beats of many of the bars; (c) there is just a slight slowing down at the end; (d) the dynamics reduce to an almost imperceptible level; (e) all the foregoing features suggest late 19th / early 20th century.

No. 8 (a) Minor, then major; (b) this is a mazurka - a mazurka is a dance in fast triple time with a tendency to accent the second beat of the bars; (c) see score; (d) see score; (e) all the foregoing answers suggest romantic period.

No. 9 (a) Major; (b) mixture of *legato* and *staccato*; (c) once, before the first very high quick notes; (d) light-hearted and witty; (e) straightforward harmony, lack of counterpoint, well-balanced phrases all suggest classical period.

No. 10 (a) Minor; (b) many duplets against triplets (see score); (b) second section slower, with a *rit.* in the middle, followed by an *a tempo*, and then a final *rit.* (d) the first section mostly single notes over an arpeggio accompaniment, the second thick block chords of some complexity; (e) the foregoing suggest the romantic period.

Printed by Caligraving Ltd.,
Brunel Way, Thetford, Norfolk. England

8/04 (52110)